The Art of Time Management

Strategies for Peak Productivity

Table of Contents

Chapter 1. Introduction

Unleash the power of every ticking second with our Special Report on "The Art of Time Management: Strategies for Peak Productivity"! We delve into the secrets of maximizing your days, mastering your schedule, and achieving your dreams in this comprehensive guide. Whether you're an ambitious individual looking to optimize working hours or a busy professional yearning for some work-life balance, this report leaves no stone unturned in transforming time from enemy to ally. Filled with cutting-edge strategies, practical insights, and inspiring stories, this Special Report is your ticket to a productive and enriching life! Get excited to conquer your 24-hour clock and start your journey to remarkable productivity now. Time waits for no one, so why should you?

Chapter 2. Reframing Your Perception of Time

Our perception of time is primarily psychological, and it flexibly adjusts according to our experiences, environment, and feelings. It's a mental construct that we often subject to association with rigidity, limitation, and undue stress. The concept of time can sometimes feel like an unyielding master dictating our lives, constantly pressuring us to do more and achieve more in less and less time. However, we can change our perspective and use it as a force, a guiding light rather than an omnipresent ticking bomb.

2.1. The Fluidity of Time Perception

Human perception of time is malleable and subject to distortions. Some minutes pass by unnoticed, while others seem endless. Ever noticed how time flies when you're engrossed in an enjoyable task? Conversely, unpleasant experiences make time seem as though it's dragging. We've all experienced relativity in time perception. Therefore, it's paramount to understand that our perception of time is not an accurate reflection of the hours, minutes, and seconds ticking away. When we realize the fluid nature of our time perception, we can begin to shed the often stress-inducing concept of rigid time, which is essential for reframing your perception of time.

2.2. From Time Management to Energy Management

The shift from seeing time as an exhaustible resource to viewing it as a way to manage your energy levels is crucial in this transformative journey. Harvard Business Review introduced a profound shift in the time management paradigm from prioritizing time to prioritizing energy. When we focus on extending our most productive hours or cramming more tasks into a packed schedule, we are not necessarily doing ourselves any favors. Rather, understanding our energy levels throughout the day, taking into account periods of activity and rest, can help us fuel productivity.

2.3. Time Abundance: An Essential Mindset Shift

Our mindset about time impacts the way we interact and use it. A 'time-scarcity' mindset is one characterized by constant striving and stress, caused by the perpetual belief that we don't have enough time. This often leads to burnout and lower productivity in the long run. On the contrary, adopting a time-abundant mindset takes you away from the scarcity principle and places you in a position to view time as a space filled with probabilities. It encourages a relaxed and confident outlook towards tasks, which fosters creativity, joy, and higher productivity.

2.4. Understanding and Identifying Time-related Stress Triggers

It is essential to understand and identify what factors related to time cause stress. It could be due dates, not having enough time, feeling unproductive, lack of relaxation or leisure time, and the likes. By identifying these triggers, you'll be better able to manage your stress and anxiety regarding time. Remember to always view these triggers as events that you can control rather than events controlling your time.

2.5. Creation versus Consumption of Time

Time can be consumed by tasks, activities, or cumbersome habits. It can also be created by actions directed towards our goals and aspirations. The activities that consume your time aren't necessarily negative; they could be routine tasks, necessary rest, or leisure. However, a balanced approach to time consumption and time creation should be fostered. Identify the activities that create and consume time and make a conscious effort to balance them in function of what you hope to achieve.

2.6. Developing Time-Centered Rituals and Habits

Developing simple, daily rituals can be a game-changer in your perception of time. Rituals or habits offer a comforting familiarity, a regularity that can reframe time from a tyrant to an ally. A morning ritual, for instance, could set the tone for the rest of your day. Likewise, an evening routine can help you wind down and prepare for a restorative sleep. Such intentional rituals encourage mindfulness and presence, strengthening your relationship with time.

In conclusion, reframing your perception of time isn't about squeezing more hours from a day. Rather, it's about harnessing the power of your mindset, your rituals, your energy levels, and your understanding of the fluidity of time to help mold your day into a canvas on which you can paint the story of your choosing. Remember, the power to make every ticking second count lies in your hands. Embrace it, and watch your productivity and contentment levels soar.

Chapter 3. The Importance of Goal Setting for Successful Time Management

The assertion that 'a goal without a plan is just a wish' cannot be overemphasized. Without clearly defined objectives and a pathway to achieve them, much energy can be wasted in happenstance activities that contribute little or nothing to the desired outcome. In essence, time management and goal setting are inseparable twins for the successful individual, both interplaying to make dreams a reality.

3.1. WHY GOAL SETTING IS VITAL IN TIME MANAGEMENT

Goal setting is the first step, the cornerstone from which efficient time management springs. It serves as the compass that guides all your planning, organization, and prioritization.

Identifying precisely what you want to achieve means you're not merely reacting to daily pressures, but proactively working towards something. Goals give you a sense of direction, purpose, and a clearer vision of what needs to be done. This has direct implications on how you spend your hours and how you choose to allocate your resources.

But above just setting those goals, they need to be SMART; Specific, Measurable, Attainable, Relevant, and Time-Bound. In other words, your objectives should not only be distinctly defined but should also be quantifiable and realistically attainable, aligned with your aspirations and have a designated timeline for completion.

3.2. THE PROCESS OF GOAL SETTING

The technique of setting goals shouldn't be hastily done, nor should it be taken lightly. It requires intentional reflection, brainstorming, and decision-making.

The first step lies in identifying what you want to achieve - these create the umbrella goals under which other activities align. These could be short-term goals, like finishing a project in a week, or long-term goals, like earning a Master's degree. A clear vision about what you want to pursue will steer your actions and decisions in the right track, filtering out non-essential tasks and distractions.

The next step is to break these goals down into manageable tasks and sub-goals. Each overarching goal can be subdivided into smaller, more manageable tasks, making the goal less intimidating and more approachable.

Then, arrange these tasks and sub-goals by their urgency and importance by applying the Eisenhower Matrix. This simple yet effective tool helps identify real priorities and weed out less essential tasks, thus further optimizing your time usage.

Next is assigning specific timelines and deadlines to your tasks. This component adds the necessary pressure and urgency needed to prevent procrastination and complacency. Deadlines serve as constant reminders of time ticking away, pushing you to act.

Finally, ensure to check in on your goals regularly, evaluating your progress and making necessary adjustments. Goal setting isn't a rigid exercise but rather a flexible process that adapts to circumstances and variations.

3.3. GOAL SETTING: A PATH TO PEAK PRODUCTIVITY

When goals are clearly defined and steps towards them are strategically organized, productivity naturally increases. With every tick of the clock, you're not groping blindly but rather progressing on a well-plotted course laced with intentionality.

Goal setting primes the mind for achievement, fine-tunes focus, and reinforces commitment. When you're focused, distractions become less enticing, and your actions become more purposeful. Plus, reaching these mini-goals fuels motivation and a sense of accomplishment, further driving productivity.

Moreover, goal setting teams up with time management to create optimal work-life balance. With well-defined goals and effective time utilization, you can work effectively within your working hours, hence creating time to relax, recreate, and rejuvenate. This invariably enhances overall productivity as your mind and body get to rest and recharge.

3.4. TACKLING OBSTACLES TO EFFECTIVE GOAL SETTING

Like any worthy pursuit, goal setting faces its own challenges such as procrastination, inappropriate goal setting, lack of motivation, etc. However, these obstacles can be nimbly handled with the right mindset and tools.

Procrastination often stems from a perception that tasks are daunting or less appealing. The way out of this quagmire often lies in breaking larger tasks into more manageable ones, creating a conducive work environment, using productivity tools, and employing simple methods like the Pomodoro technique to keep work engaging and less straining.

On the other hand, many fall into the pitfall of setting inappropriate or unrealistic goals. The key to unlocking this trap lies in setting SMART goals that inspire rather than intimidate.

Furthermore, staying motivated can often be a rollercoaster. Remember that motivation often follows action, not the other way round. Therefore, kickstart your tasks, and you'll find the motivation picking up as you progress.

All said, goal setting remains the foundation upon which successful time management systems are built. It empowers control over your life, provides clarity and focus, enhances decision-making, and propels you towards your desired future. By marrying goal setting with effective time management strategies, you not only conquer the 24 hours at your disposal but, more importantly, step confidently into the life of your dreams.

Chapter 4. Maximizing Productivity: The Power of Prioritization

The most successful individuals all have one thing in common: they understand the power of prioritization. This skill, more than any other, will set you on the path to peak productivity and fulfilment. Now, it's time for you to unlock this power.

We'll begin by exploring the rationale behind prioritization and why it's crucial for every activity, no matter how minor or grand. Following that, we will discuss the tactics you can utilize to prioritize effectively. We'll finally finish with actionable strategies to overcome possible hurdles during the prioritization process.

4.1. The Rationale Behind Prioritization

It's human nature to desire accomplishment—the satisfaction of crossing items off a to-do list. But, the problem arises when the list grows and diversifies, encompassing both simple tasks and awe-inspiring goals. It can leave one overwhelmed and, often, paralysed. The solution? Prioritization—separating the important from the trivial and focusing on what truly matters.

On the surface, prioritization might seem like a simple task. Yet, it's akin to distilling a wide array of ambitions and responsibilities into actionable tasks that align with your long-term objectives. In this sense, it mirrors pruning a tree—you remove the unproductive branches to allow the tree (your life and work) to flourish.

4.2. Techniques for Prioritizing

Mastering prioritization involves two intricately woven steps: classifying tasks based on their importance and urgency and then determining the correct action depending on the category.

Let's break this down:

1. **Categorization**: Renowned president and productivity enthusiast Dwight D. Eisenhower developed a grid dubbed as the Eisenhower Matrix or Eisenhower Box. This consists of four quarters, which allow you to classify tasks as `Urgent and Important`, `Important but Not Urgent`, `Urgent but Not Important`, and `Neither Urgent nor Important`.

2. **Action Plan**: After classifying, it's time for action. Tasks that are both important and urgent require immediate attention. Tasks deemed important, but not urgent, should be scheduled for later. If a task is urgent but not important, see if it can be delegated. If it's neither urgent nor important, it could potentially be eliminated.

It's essential to apply the Eisenhower Matrix from a bird's eye perspective, i.e., in the context of your overarching goals. An `Important` task isn't simply one that demands a lot of time or resources; instead, it's one that aligns with your goals.

4.3. Overcoming Prioritization Roadblocks

Effective prioritization is not without its challenges and pitfalls. Let's look at how to navigate these to stay on your productivity path.

1. **Hurry Sickness**: This is the tendency to assume everything is urgent and requires immediate completion. Counter it by

routinely reminding yourself of your fundamental goals. One technique is to keep your goals visibly placed somewhere you frequently see, such as a desktop wallpaper or a sticky note on your work desk.

2. **Perfectionism**: Craving to make everything perfect can be counterproductive. It often leads to spending excess time on tasks of lesser importance. Know when to say 'good enough' and move on to the next task on your priority list.

3. **Procrastination**: This common issue often strikes when faced with daunting tasks. Break down such tasks into smaller, manageable ones. Then tackle them one by one, starting with the most challenging portion first when your energy levels are at a peak.

4. **Lack of Motivation**: This can result from a mismatch between your tasks and your fundamental aspirations. If you frequently find yourself tackling tasks that don't align with your personal goals, it might be time for some introspection and realignment.

Remember, prioritization isn't merely about identifying the most critical tasks. It's about recognizing and eliminating the least productive ones—and understanding that sometimes, it's okay to say 'no'. Prioritization, in essence, is equivalent to setting boundaries. Not merely boundaries that protect your time, but that safeguard your peace of mind and forge a path to peak productivity.

Happy prioritizing! May your time be filled with fruitful work and endeavors that align with your dreams. As you start applying these strategies, you will gradually witness significant changes. Your tasks will align better with your goals, leading to satisfaction that extends beyond mere `productivity`.

Not only will mastering the art of prioritization improve your productivity, it will also, and perhaps more importantly, drastically improve the quality of your life. After all, true productivity rests in doing more of what really matters.

Chapter 5. Effective Planning: Your Blueprint for Success

To unlock the magic of effective time management, comprehensive and strategic planning is indispensable. It serves as the blueprint, guiding you from point A — where you are currently — to point B — your ultimate goals and dreams. Achieving success without a solid plan is akin to sailing a ship without a compass; you'll likely go adrift.

5.1. Understanding the Importance of Planning

Planning lays the groundwork for taking control of your time. It allows you to visualize your objectives and the necessary steps to reach there. This process requires precision, analysis, and attention to detail. A well-formulated plan is a portfolio of your goals, strategies, and timelines — a clear road map steering you towards success.

A lack of planning often results in mismanaged time, crisis-driven work patterns, and unmet objectives. Pooling in time to plan consequently saves more time by eliminating confusion, reducing errors, and ensuring each activity is intentionally directed towards achieving your desired outcome.

5.2. Setting S.M.A.R.T Goals

The initial step in planning is crystallizing what you aim to accomplish with your time — setting goals. For effective planning and enhanced productivity, it's crucial to set S.M.A.R.T — Specific, Measurable, Achievable, Relevant, and Time-bound — goals.

-Specific: Ensure your goals are well-defined, clear, and

unambiguous. -Measurable: Quantify your goals so that progress can be tracked. -Achievable: Set realistic goals that are achievable within your resources and capabilities. -Relevant: Align your goals with your long-term objectives and aspirations. -Time-bound: Assign a definite timeline to achieve each goal.

Such goal setting offers a clear sense of direction, increased focus, and forthcoming sense of accomplishment.

5.3. Mapping Out a Plan

Once you've set your S.M.A.R.T goals, devising a well-structured plan is the next crucial step.

1. Analyze the tasks: Break down your goal into smaller, manageable tasks. Understanding the strength, potential roadblocks, and interdependencies of each task will help you strategize better.

2. Prioritize the tasks: Not all tasks are created equal. Use the Eisenhower Matrix, or other prioritization tools, to decide on the tasks' urgency and importance.

3. Allocate resources: Enlist the resources needed for each task, including time, people, money, and materials.

5.4. Creating a Timeline

An effective plan includes not just what needs to be done, but also when. To ensure your goals are time-bound, creating a timeline is indispensable.

1. Determine the deadline: Start by defining the ultimate due date.

2. Assign dates to individual tasks: Break down your goal and assign a stretch of time to each task, keeping their importance and urgency in mind.

3. Allow for contingencies: Things rarely go exactly as planned. Design your timeline with some leeway for unexpected delays and amend it if required.

5.5. Implementing the Plan

As important as creating the plan is implementing it. Sticking to your plan will help you harness time to your advantage.

1. Maintain discipline: Execute the plan as per the timeline and resist the urge to procrastinate.

2. Stay focused: Concentrate on the task at hand, avoiding multitasking as far as possible.

3. Regularly review progress: Monitoring your progress can motivate you and help you make necessary adjustments on time.

5.6. Coping with Obstacles

The path to success is rarely smooth. You may encounter various obstacles in the course of your plan implementation.

1. Problem-solving: Adopt a solution-oriented mindset rather than dwelling on the problem.

2. Flexibility: Don't hesitate to tweak the plan to navigate successfully through unexpected events.

3. Resilience: Keep an unwavering focus on your goals; temporary setbacks should not deter your spirits.

In conclusion, effective planning is your sure-shot way to optimize your available time and secure success. It structures your life, gives you a glimpse of what's ahead, and provides a foolproof strategy to reach your goals. As you begin incorporating these strategies into your life, you'll notice a significant increase in your productivity and an incredible transformation in your approach towards time. Time management, after all, is not just about managing your time; it's about managing your life.

Remember, "Failing to plan is planning to fail." So, plan wisely, and soon, you'll see your path to success becoming clearer and less challenging. Make planning an indispensable part of your life, and let it lead you to the pinnacle of productivity.

Chapter 6. Delegation: Leveraging Teamwork for Enhanced Productivity

Delegation is often touted as a critical skill in leadership and management. Yet, surprisingly few professionals are adept at this art. True delegation is more than just assigning tasks; it involves empowering your team to operate at their highest potential.

One of the hurdles to successful delegation is the misconception that it equates to shirking work and responsibility. The contrary couldn't be more accurate: effective delegation helps create a productive, collaborative work environment where team members are encouraged to learn, grow, and innovate. Let's dive into how delegation can become your game-changer for enhanced productivity.

6.1. Understanding Delegation

At its core, delegation is about optimally distributing responsibilities among team members to accomplish a common goal. It leverages diversity, creativity, and specialization to achieve an outcome potentially greater than the sum of its parts.

Delegation consists of key elements:

- Assigning tasks: This is perhaps the most familiar aspect of delegation. It involves identifying tasks within a project or process and assigning them to different team members or collaborative units.

- Sharing authority: Once tasks are assigned, the accompanying authority must also be shared, allowing individuals or teams to make decisions relevant to their tasks without constant supervision. This independence infuses team members with a sense of ownership for their work.

- Maintaining responsibility: Although tasks and authority are shared, the overall responsibility remains with the person delegating. This means they should monitor progress, provide support and guidance when necessary, and ensure that the work is completed effectively and timely.

6.2. The Importance of Delegation

Delegation boosts productivity both at individual and team levels. Here's how:

- Freeing up Time: Delegation allows managers to focus on strategic tasks by passing operational tasks to team members. This can contribute significantly to meeting organizational goals.

- Employee Motivation and Development: Delegating responsibilities boosts employee morale. It signals trust in their abilities while providing opportunities for new skills development.

- Enhanced Efficiency: Tasks are completed more quickly and efficiently when assigned to team members with specific skills related to said tasks.

- Collaborative Climate: Delegation encourages a cooperative work environment, fostering innovation and creative problem-solving.

6.3. Strategies for Effective Delegation

While recognizing the importance of delegation is the first step, mastering the nuances of its application is crucial. Here are strategies to make the process effective.

- Know Your Team: Allocate time to understand the strengths, weaknesses, interests, and capabilities of your team members. This knowledge will help assign tasks to the right individuals.

- Clear Communication: Provide comprehensive information about the task, including objectives, deadlines, and resources. Ensure that the team members understand what is expected of them.

- Delegate Authority: Ensure that team members can make decisions about their tasks to avoid delays and unnecessary consultations. However, they should also be made aware of the limits of their authority.

- Provide Support: Delegation does not mean absence. Be available for guidance and support. Feedback, both positive and corrective, is crucial.

6.4. Overcoming Barriers to Delegation

Several issues can hinder successful delegation.

- Fear of Losing Control: Some managers worry that by delegating, they lose control over the work. This can be countered by setting performance standards, monitoring progress, and building trust with the team.

- Fear of Work Being Done Poorly: There's always the risk of tasks being completed suboptimally. However, this can be minimized by allocating tasks based on team capabilities and providing support and guidance.

- Inadequate Delegation Skills: A simple solution here is training. Managers can be taught effective delegation techniques to enhance both their skills and confidence.

Delegation is an invaluable skill for any leader, manager, or ambitious professional. Possessing the ability to distribute duties effectively and responsibly allows you to focus on higher-level tasks and goals. Most importantly, it cultivates a positive and developmental atmosphere within your team, fueling collaboration, innovation, and success.

By understanding and applying the strategies presented here, delegation can become the linchpin for maximizing productivity and creating thriving, proactive teams. It's time to embrace delegation as not merely a task-assignment tool but a productivity multiplier and a leverage point for sustainable success.

Chapter 7. Procrastination: The Enemy Within and How to Overcome It

Every fleeting moment is a formidable test that determines whether we can press on, or yield to the temptation that pleases our immediate sense of comfort. Procrastination is undoubtedly one of the biggest roadblocks to productivity. It sabotages our time management efforts, resulting in missed deadlines, reduced quality of work, and increased stress.

7.1. Understanding the Trap of Procrastination

Firstly, we need to understand what we're dealing with. Procrastination is not just a matter of poor time management; it's the deliberate delay of tasks that we find challenging, uninteresting, or overwhelming. It's a habit that feeds on our fears and anxieties.

Cognitive scientists regard procrastination as a mechanism of the brain to avoid unpleasant tasks. When we feel an instinctive dread in tackling a daunting task, our minds are wired to seek instant gratification, preferring simpler tasks over the more critical ones.

7.2. The Impact of Procrastination

Procrastination is not a benign habit, but a seemingly harmless enemy that can erode one's productivity and drain mental well-being. When procrastination becomes a habit, it inhibits peak productivity, derails progress and adversely affects our reputation and relationships.

By chronic procrastination, the procrastinator constantly feels stressed due to the impending undone tasks. The irony here is the more they worry, the less likely they are to begin. This stress inhibits the capacity to perform optimally, and can result in mental and physical health problems in the long run.

7.3. The Psychology Behind Procrastination

Research has unveiled three psychological factors that contribute markedly to procrastination: fear, perfectionism, and self-efficacy.

Fear is undoubtedly a strong motivator for procrastination, particularly the fear of failure. When people fear the outcome of a task, they tend to put it off. Yet, by dodging it, they actually foster this fear.

Perfectionism is another root cause. Perfectionists often delay starting a task because they dread not being able to complete it flawlessly.

Self-efficacy refers to one's belief in their ability to succeed in specific situations or accomplish a task. Low self-efficacy leads to a lack of confidence in one's skills, increasing the chances of procrastination.

7.4. Strategies to Overcome Procrastination

Simply understanding procrastination and its implications isn't enough. We must actively fight it. Here are some science-backed strategies to overcome this enemy within.

7.4.1. Break it Down

Breaking down a task into smaller, more manageable bits can help make a daunting task less intimidating. We feel a sense of accomplishment when we complete each small task, which motivates us to proceed to the next one.

7.4.2. The Pomodoro Technique

Francesco Cirillo's Pomodoro Technique is a time management method intended to defeat procrastination. The technique suggests working for 25-minute intervals, separated by short five-minute breaks, and taking a longer break every four "Pomodoros".

7.4.3. Acceptance and Commitment Therapy (ACT)

ACT is a form of mindfulness-based therapy that encourages people to embrace their thoughts and feelings rather than fighting or feeling guilty for them. It can be greatly helpful in overcoming procrastination by accepting the inherent discomfort of a task and committing to completing them.

7.4.4. Building Self-Efficacy

Strengthen your self-belief. Start by tackling smaller tasks to gradually build your confidence. As your self-efficacy improves, your proclivity for procrastination decreases.

7.4.5. Time Boxing

Allocating a definite time slot for a task, known as time boxing, can be effective in combating procrastination. Instead of focusing on task completion, the goal is to commit a specific amount of time to the task.

7.4.6. Eliminate Distractions

In the digital age, distractions proliferate, making it harder to maintain focus. Cultivate an environment that enables concentration. Turn off notifications, create a dedicated workspace, or use applications that limit time on social media platforms.

Procrastination, if left unchecked, can be crippling. But with the right mindset and tools, we can conquer this insidious enemy. Remember, every moment is an opportunity for action. By harnessing these moments, you harness your life. Embrace the challenge, seize the moment, and eliminate procrastination. Because, as they say, time waits for no one!

The battle with procrastination is not fought in a day but won over time with consistent effort. Adopt these strategies to conquer procrastination and unlock your full productivity potential. However, it's important to remember that occasionally giving in to procrastination is not the end of the world. What matters is progress, not perfection, in our ongoing journey towards greater productivity and fulfillment.

Chapter 8. Striking the Perfect Work-Life Balance

Understanding the importance of a healthy work-life balance is a cornerstone to anyone's success - personal or professional. Balancing the tasks of work with our personal lives is akin to walking on a tightrope. Too often, the scales tip one way or the other, resulting in overwork and burnout or loss of focus and underperformance. A harmonious work-life balance not only adds to productivity but also yields a satisfying and fulfilling life.

8.1. Setting Boundaries

A large part of striking an optimal work-life balance involves the establishment of boundaries. These boundaries must be set both on a professional as well as personal level.

For professionals, the line that differentiates work and non-work activities could blur, especially in an age where remote work and virtual offices are the norm. Joys of flexible work can easily transform into the burden of 'always being on.' In light of this, adhering strictly to set work hours and resisting the temptation to peek at that email late at night can help maintain your peace of mind and relaxation time. Remember, work will always be there tomorrow.

Conversely, during work hours, minimize personal engagements as much as possible. Use your work hours efficiently. Cultivating discipline and focus can be a potent tool in managing your time effectively, which will, in turn, leave more time for personal engagements.

8.2. Importance of Downtime

"Idle time is not wasted time," goes the saying. Incorporating downtime into your schedule serves to rejuvenate your mind, sparks creativity, and enhances productivity. Take short breaks during work, engage in activities you enjoy, meditate, or simply go for a short walk. Unplugging is crucial to maintaining mental health and ensuring better concentration when you return to work.

It's essential to have full days where you do not engage in work-related activities as well. Use these rest days to pursue a hobby, socialize, or simply to relax. The change of pace and focus will help you come back to work more refreshed and invigorated.

8.3. Scheduling Personal Time

We schedule our work hours meticulously. Why should personal time be any different? Allocate time slots for activities like exercise, reading, family time, and personal growth. This approach ensures the non-negotiable events of your life are given as much importance as your work-related tasks.

8.4. Delegation and Prioritization

Delegation liberates not only your time but also your mental space. Delegate tasks that do not require your sole attention or expertise. This shift allows you to concentrate on tasks that require your unique set of skills and expertise and saves time and energy, making the workload manageable.

Crafting a daily or weekly to-do list helps keep track of tasks and prioritize based on urgency and importance. Use the Eisenhower Box, a simple decision-making tool that helps prioritize. Utilize this time-honored strategy to sift through tasks and differentiate between what's urgent, not urgent, important, or not important.

8.5. Embrace Flexibility

An essential part of achieving work-life balance is to remain flexible. Life occurs, and sometimes things do not go as planned. A healthy work-life balance involves the ability to be adaptable and not becoming overly frustrated when our timetable is disrupted.

Although our correlation should be time-bound, we must also learn to accommodate changes. While flexibility can seem conflicting with setting boundaries, setting boundaries isn't a rigid structure but rather a framework that allows for necessary adjustments.

8.6. Include Wellness Activities

Good physical health is a cornerstone of overall well-being and impacts your capacity in both personal and professional arenas. Biologically, exercise releases endorphins that elevate mood and have been linked with improved cognitive function, which can boost your work productivity.

Eating healthy provides necessary fuel for your daily activities. Good nutrition paired with regular exercise bolsters your immune system, keeping you healthy and active.

Quality sleep is as critical as healthy eating and regular exercise. Lack of sleep can lead to physical health issues like increased risk of heart diseases and mental health problems like anxiety and depression. It also affects productivity, concentration, and weight.

A healthy work-life balance involves balancing the trinity of wellness- exercise, nutrition, and sleep to ensure you are at your physical and mental best.

8.7. Support Work-Life Balance Culture

Make sure your organization values work-life balance. An organizational culture that encourages its employees to disconnect after work hours, takes mental health seriously, rewards efficiency as opposed to long hours, and provides flexibility can contribute heavily to achieving a work-life balance.

In conclusion, striking the perfect work-life balance is a continuous, conscious process. It is not a one-time task but needs regular reassessment and adjustment. It's not a destination, but a journey to be enjoyed.

Chapter 9. Leveraging Modern Tools for Time Management

As we embrace the digital era, leveraging modern tools for time management has become more necessary than ever. The beauty of these tools lies in their capacity to automatize processes and provide efficient systems to better organize your tasks and projects. In exploring these tools, we aim to provide you with an array of options to streamline your workflow, thereby enhancing productivity.

9.1. Harnessing the Power of Time Management Tools

Digital tools for time management encapsulate a broad spectrum of utilities, ranging from calendars and to-do lists to project management softwares, all with one common goal – to help you manage your time wisely and efficiently.

Among the plethora of tools available, let's start with a tool that has become a cornerstone in contemporary time management – digital calendars. Among the most popular are Google Calendar, Microsoft Outlook, and Apple Calendar. These tools integrate smoothly with other applications, allowing you to synchronize tasks, deadlines, appointments, and email notifications. The added functionality of setting reminders ensures that no task goes forgotten.

To-do list applications also serve as crucial tools in modern time management. Tools like Asana, Trello, and Todoist enable you to categorize tasks, set priorities, and track progress. The visualization they provide makes it easier to approach tasks methodically, thereby enhancing productivity by reducing the time and effort associated with task management.

The concept of task batching can be significantly facilitated by time blocking tools. Among these, Plan and TimeTune stand out. They help you allocate blocks of time to specific tasks or categories of tasks, helping ensure that your focus remains undivided for that period. This method of scheduling tasks reduces the mental fatigue associated with context switching between different tasks.

9.2. Embracing Project Management Tools for Enhanced Productivity

When it comes to managing large projects, project management tools come in handy. Tools like Basecamp, Monday.com, Jira, and Slack encapsulate features such as task assignment, progress tracking, and collaboration which can help in managing large teams and projects. The ability to oversee an entire project from a single platform ensures everyone stays in the loop and synchronized, which in turn pays dividends in productivity.

Another tool gaining traction in the project management arena is Notion. This all-in-one workspace allows for note-taking, database handling, project management, and more. It effectively acts as a knowledge sharing platform, enabling teams to centralize their work in one accessible space.

9.3. Exploring the World of Automated Tools for Streamlined Workflow

In the age of automation, failure to leverage automated tools can mean missed opportunities in optimizing time usage. Automation tools such as Zapier, IFTTT (If This Then That), and Microsoft Power

Automate work by creating automated workflows between applications. These tools can automate repetitive tasks, leaving you with more time to focus on complex and impactful activities.

For example, if you're using social media for your business or personal brand, tools like Buffer or Hootsuite allow you to schedule posts weeks in advance. Similarly, tools like Mailchimp can automate email newsletters and marketing campaigns.

Moreover, if you deal with a lot of paperwork, a tool like Adobe Sign or DocuSign can revolutionize your workflow. These tools allow you to sign, send, and manage documents digitally, thereby significantly reducing paper-related clutter and saving time in the process.

9.4. Utilizing AI Technology for Time Management

Ai technology is a rising star in the realm of time management tools. Ai personal assistants such as Google Assistant, Siri, and Alexa can perform various tasks such as setting reminders, taking notes, and even sending emails. Furthermore, Ai powered tools such as x.ai and Clara can automate the task of scheduling meetings by handling email correspondences on your behalf.

To fully exploit these modern tools, it is essential to determine which ones best align with your specific needs and work style. Remember, the goal here is to enhance your productivity by efficiently managing your time, not to be overwhelmed by the tools themselves.

9.5. Conclusion: The Future of Time Management

As technology keeps evolving, newer and more sophisticated tools continue to emerge. It is clear that the future of time management lies in our ability to adapt and make the best use of these tools. After all, the ultimate aim is to increase productivity and hence, the quality of life.

So begin your exploration today! Choose the right tools to augment your time management skills, transform your productivity, and seize control of your 24-hour clock. Time waits for no one, and neither should you!

Chapter 10. Cultivating a Productive Mindset

The first, and arguably the most crucial step towards achieving peak productivity, is to cultivate a productive mindset. Your mindset is a key determinant of not only your productivity but also your happiness, success, and overall quality of life. A mindset is a set of assumptions, methods, and notions held by an individual or exercised by a group. It impacts how you perceive yourself and the world around you.

Understanding the Role of Mindset ===

Psychologist Carol Dweck, a pioneer in mindset research, brought the concept of "growth mindset" and "fixed mindset" to the forefront of psychological study. According to her, individuals with a fixed mindset believe their abilities are static and immutable. In contrast, those with a growth mindset view challenges as opportunities to expand their skills and knowledge.

In the context of productivity, cultivating a growth mindset is vital. It allows you to embrace challenges, persist in the face of setbacks, see effort as the path to mastery, and learn from criticism.

Setting Your Mind in the Productivity Direction ===

Cultivating a productive mindset isn't about working harder; it's about working smarter. It's about creating an inner environment where your thoughts, attitudes, and beliefs are aligned in a way that makes productivity a natural outcome. Here are five strategies to help set your mind in the 'productivity direction.'

1. Define Your Vision: Knowing your purpose is the starting point of all achievement. By clearly defining what you want to accomplish, you set in motion the force of directed action that

leads to transformation and success.

2. Establish SMART Goals: SMART stands for Specific, Measurable, Achievable, Relevant, and Time-Bound. Setting SMART goals ensures you have clear objectives to strive towards and provides a framework for managing your time and resources efficiently.

3. Emphasize Positivity and Possibility: A positive mindset nurtures productive energies. By focusing on possibilities instead of limitations, you're more likely to take constructive action toward your goals.

4. Nurture Self-Discipline: Productivity springs from discipline—the discipline to prioritize, to work instead of procrastinating, and to maintain focus despite distractions. Cultivating self-discipline paves the way for forming and maintaining productive habits.

5. Continual Learning: Adopt a 'learner's mindset.' Keeping an open mind to acquire new knowledge and skills continually ensures you're well-equipped to overcome productivity roadblocks.

Transforming Thoughts into Action ===

Once you have adopted the right set of attitudes and beliefs geared toward productivity, the next phase is to translate these thoughts into action. Here are four strategies to effectively transform your mindset into measurable productivity.

1. Implement a Productivity System: One of the best ways to manifest a productive mindset is to deploy an organizing system. Various tactics, such as time boxing, the Pomodoro Technique, or getting things done (GTD) model, can guide your workflow.

2. Cultivate Productive Habits and Rituals: Develop a set of rituals that signal your brain it's time to settle into deep work, such as meditating in the morning or maintaining a tidy workspace. These habits and rituals can make a significant difference in sustaining your productivity throughout the day.

3. Harness the Power of Technology: Utilize productivity apps to

coordinate your tasks and manage your time. There are excellent digital tools available that can help you stay organized and focused.

4. Practice Mindfulness: Mindfulness increases awareness, enabling you to notice when you're getting off track and reorient your focus towards productivity.

Maintaining Your Productive Mindset ===

Cultivating a productive mindset is not a one-time task, but an ongoing journey. Here are three strategies to help you maintain your productivity-focused mindset over time.

1. Regular Review and Reflection: Regular time spent reflecting on your productivity enables you to monitor your progress, identify bottlenecks, and refine your strategies.

2. Seek Feedback: Regularly seeking feedback from peers, mentors, or coaches can provide you with an external perspective and insight into areas that could be improved.

3. Celebrate Accomplishments: Celebrating achievements, regardless of size, can help you stay motivated and remind you of the progress you've made on your productivity journey.

Every tick of the clock is a testament to the power of time—a resource that, once lost, we cannot reclaim. Thus, understanding and using this power wisely lies at the crux of productivity. Cultivating a productive mindset provides the motivational energy, strategic vision, and resilient spirit you need to make the most of every moment.

Remember; productivity isn't about being busy. It's about fulfilling your commitments, transforming your dreams into reality, and living your best life. Your mindset is the seed, productivity the tree, and your fulfilled ambitions, the lush fruits. Nurture this seed, and the tree of productivity will stand robustly in the forest of your life, bearing you fruits of success and satisfaction.

Chapter 11. Resilience and Flexibility: Adapting to Unforeseen Circumstances

Our journey begins with understanding a powerful and fundamental aspect of successful time management—the ability to be resilient and flexible.

In life, and particularly in today's fast-paced society, our schedules are subject to constant pressure. From simple things like traffic congestion to more signifiant events like a sudden business crisis, unexpected events can strike causing disruption at any time. It's how we react to these curveballs that strongly influences our productivity and overall success in life. Ideally, we want to relieve and manage stress that accompanies unforeseen circumstances, bounce back with resolve, and adapt our plans swiftly and strategically. This is where resilience and flexibility come into play.

11.1. The Dual Art of Resilience and Flexibility

Resilience is typically defined as the ability to recover quickly from difficulties. It is about persistence and determination to keep going, to chart a new course of action when the current one becomes untenable.

Flexibility, on the other hand, refers to the ability to adapt effectively to new circumstances. It involves being open to change and having the capacity to modify or adjust one's thoughts and behaviors in response to the demands of a situation.

While closely linked, resilience and flexibility serve different functions. You can think of resilience as the engine driving us forward during trials and tribulations, while flexibility is the navigation system, guiding us on an adapted course when roadblocks emerge. To optimize your time and life, mastering both these skills is crucial.

11.2. Building Robust Resilience

Building resilience is a proactive process, not a reactive one. Here are a handful of strategies that have been scientifically proven to enhance this ability:

1. Maintain a Positive Outlook: A positive mindset can equip you with the motivation to overcome obstacles and identify opportunities where others might only see failure.

2. Forge Strong Social Connections: Relationships can serve as a protective buffer against life's stressors. A strong support network can offer objective advice, nurture your confidence, and keep you grounded.

3. Embrace Change: See changes as a normal part of life and as gateways to new opportunities.

4. Nurture Mental and Physical Health: Regular physical activity, a balanced diet, and mindfulness practices go a long way in maintaining your overall well-being, which, in turn, makes you more resilient.

5. Never Stop Learning: Face your challenges as a transformational learning experience. Utilize every setback to improve and grow.

Note that resilience is a skill; it can be learned and practiced over time.

"===" Developing Fluid Flexibility

Being flexible involves adjusting to new conditions with ease. Below, we outline strategies to facilitate and enhance flexibility:

1. Foster Openness: Welcome new experiences and perspectives. Diverse thought processes can help in the adaptation of different strategies, a key attribute of flexibility.

2. Practice Empathy: Trying to understand other's perspectives can allow more flexibility in thinking.

3. Equip Yourself with Knowledge: Educate yourself across wide-ranging topics. The broader your knowledge, the more flexible you can be as you'll have more alternatives to choose from when you need to rethink your strategy.

4. Move Beyond Comfort Zones: Step out of your comfort zone and accept the discomfort of new situations. It will assist in developing flexibility over time.

5. Be Future Ready: Actively predict and prepare for various possible futures, even if they seem unlikely at the moment.

Much like resilience, flexibility too is a learnable skill that one can nurture with conscious effort.

11.3. Balancing Resilience and Flexibility

When coupled together, resilience and flexibility become a powerhouse of an individual's time management toolkit. However, the important trick lies in maintaining a balance. Too much resilience could lead to stubborn adherence to outmoded strategies, whereas excessive flexibility could result in indecisiveness due to an abundance of options. Therefore, establish resilience to stay motivated through trials, while leveraging flexibility to make adjustments when necessary.

11.4. Unanticipated Circumstances: Harnessing Resilience and Flexibility

Consider a project that suddenly encounters a critical roadblock. Use resilience to maintain optimism that there is a path towards completion. Flexibility, on the other hand, will aid adjusting project plans to circumvent the roadblock effectively.

Both resilience and flexibility have the potential to convert unanticipated setbacks into opportunities for growth. The capacity to devise alternate plans and carry them out with enthusiasm, even in the face of adversity, is what separates peak performers from the rest.

As we conclude this chapter, remember that resilience and flexibility often require courage: courage to perceive change, not as a threat but as a thrilling opportunity; courage to stand up when knocked down; and courage to tune into shifting winds and adjust your sails. With resilience and flexibility in your arsenal, you can manage your time more effectively and navigate the sea of life with an unwavering spirit. Make the leap, and remember, fortune favors the brave.

www.ingramcontent.com/pod-product-compliance
Lightning Source LLC
Chambersburg PA
CBHW071049260726

48661CB00007B/3232